THE
WORD
DETECTIVE
IN GERMAN

First published in 1982
Usborne Publishing Ltd
83-85 Saffron Hill
London EC1N 8RT, England

© Usborne Publishing Ltd 1982

Printed in Great Britain

The name of Usborne and the device are trademarks of Usborne Publishing Ltd.

The Word Detectives

A Noun is the name of anything. It can be the name of a thing, like a <u>door</u>, a place like a <u>castle</u> or a person, like a <u>man</u>.

Inspektor Nomen
Inspector Noun

A Verb is always busy and tells you about what is happening. <u>Walks</u>, <u>runs</u> and <u>barks</u> are all Verbs.

Wachtmeister Verb
Sergeant Verb

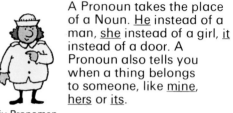

A Pronoun takes the place of a Noun. <u>He</u> instead of a man, <u>she</u> instead of a girl, <u>it</u> instead of a door. A Pronoun also tells you when a thing belongs to someone, like <u>mine</u>, <u>hers</u> or <u>its</u>.

Detektiv Pronomen
Detective Pronoun

An Adjective tells you something else about a noun. The words underlined are adjectives: a <u>green</u> door, a <u>tall</u> man, an <u>old</u> castle.

Detektiv Adjektiv
Detective Adjective

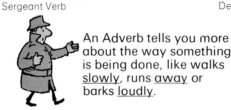

An Adverb tells you more about the way something is being done, like walks <u>slowly</u>, runs <u>away</u> or barks <u>loudly</u>.

Detektiv Adverb
Detective Adverb

A Preposition goes before a Noun or Pronoun and tells you more about them, such as <u>behind</u> the man, <u>into</u> the castle, or the dog went <u>with</u> him.

Detektiv Präposition
Detective Preposition

About this book

This book is for everyone learning German. By looking at the pictures, it will be easy to read and learn the words and sentences.

Masculine, feminine and neuter words

When you look at the German words, you will see that most of them have **der, die** or **das**, which means "the", in front of them. This is because in German all words, like airport or cave, as well as man and woman, are masculine or feminine, and some words, like car, are neuter. **Der** means the word is masculine, **die** means that it is feminine, and **das** means it is neuter. **Die** is also the word for "the" before plural words. They are marked in the pictures with a *

Looking at the words

You will see that many German words start with a capital, or big, letter. There is also the letter ß in some words which sounds the same as "ss". On some vowels there are two dots, **ä, ö, ü**. This is called an umlaut and changes the sound of the vowel.

Saying the words

At the back of the book there are guides to pronouncing all the words and sentences on the pictures. These are to help you say them. But there are some sounds in German that are quite different from any sound in English. To say them as a German person would, you have to hear them spoken and say them like that yourself.

Translating the sentences

When you look at the English translation of the German sentences, you will see that the words do not always match. This is because in German sometimes the words are in a different order, sometimes there are more or less words, and some things are said in a different way. If you translated the sentences word for word, you would have very strange English.

Spot the mouse

On every picture across two pages there is a mouse. Can you find it?

THE
WORD
DETECTIVE
IN GERMAN
With Easy Pronunciation Guide

Heather Amery and Sonja Osthecker
Illustrated by Colin King

Pronunciation Guide by Gillian Adams

Inspektor Nomen und die geheimnisvollen Vorgänge auf dem Markt

Inspector Noun and the market mystery

der Markt

das Gemüse   **das Obst**

Nomen geht auf den Markt, um einen Dieb zu finden.
Noun goes to market to find a thief.

die Kirschen*

Er denkt: „Wer ißt die Kirschen
He thinks, "Who is eating the cherries

die Erdbeeren*

und die Erdbeeren
and the strawberries

die Himbeeren*

und die Himbeeren?"
and the raspberries?"

die Ananas

Er sieht sich eine Ananas an,
He looks at a pineapple,

die Melone

läßt eine Melone fallen
drops a melon

der Apfel

und ißt einen Apfel.
and eats an apple.

die Orangen*

Er geht an den Orangen,
He walks past the oranges,

die Zitronen*

den Zitronen
the lemons

die Aprikosen*

und den Aprikosen vorbei.
and the apricots.

die Birnen*

Er schaut die Birnen,
He looks at the pears,

die Trauben*

die Trauben
at the grapes

die Bananen*

und die Bananen an.
and the bananas.

der Pfirsich

die Pampelmuse

die Pflaumen*

Er bleibt stehen, um auf einen Pfirsich zu drücken und um eine Pampelmuse und ein Paar Pflaumen zu
He stops to squeeze a peach,   buy a grapefruit   and some plums.   **kaufen.**

4

die Erbsen*

„Wer hat die Erbsen
"Who has been eating the peas

die Bohnen*

und die Bohnen
and the beans

der Salat

und den Salat gegessen?"
and the lettuce?"

die Kartoffeln*

Nomen untersucht die Kartoffeln
Noun looks at the potatoes

die Möhren*

und die Möhren
and the carrots

die Kohlköpfe*

und die Kohlköpfe.
and the cabbages.

die Tomate

Er tritt auf eine Tomate,
He steps on a tomato,

die Pilze*

stößt ein Körbchen voller Pilze
knocks down some mushrooms

die Wasserkresse

und einen Eimer mit Wasserkresse um.
and kicks over the watercress.

die Rüben*

Er schaut hinter den Rüben
He peers round the turnips

der Rosenkohl

und dem Rosenkohl hervor
and the sprouts

die Rote Bete

und kriecht an der Roten Bete vorbei.
and crawls past the beetroot.

die Sellerie

Er geht an der Sellerie vorbei,
He walks past the celery,

die Radieschen*

und sieht sich die Radieschen
and looks at the radishes

die Zwiebeln*

und die Zwiebeln an.
and the onions.

der Lauch

Er rutscht auf einer Lauch aus,
He slips on a leek,

der Blumenkohl

stolpert über einen Blumenkohl
trips over a cauliflower

die Diebe*

und findet die Diebe.
and finds the thieves.

Inspektor Nomen und die gestohlenen Diamanten
Inspector Noun and the stolen diamonds

das Schiff

Inspektor Nomen fährt zu dem Schiff.
Inspector Noun drives to the ship.

das Fallreep

Er geht das Fallreep hinauf
He walks up the gang plank

der Kapitän

und spricht mit dem Kapitän.
and talks to the captain.

die Diamanten*

der Dieb

die Frau

Der Kapitän erzählt ihm, daß einige Diamanten von einem Dieb gestohlen worden sind. Aber eine Frau
The captain says some diamonds have been stolen by a thief. But a woman saw him. hat ihn gesehen

die Flagge

die Winde

das Deck

der Matrose

die Luke

die Kette

die Schiffskatze

der Anker

die Fracht

der Laderaum

die Koje

die Mannschafts-kabine

die Kabine

der Bug

der Maschinenraum

6

das Deck

Nomen schleicht über das Deck
Noun creeps along the deck

der Mann

und fängt den Mann.
and catches the man.

die Taschen*

Aber seine Taschen sind leer.
But his pockets are empty.

Der Dieb hat die Diamanten auf dem Schiff versteckt.
Kannst du sie finden?
The thief has hidden the diamonds in the ship.
Can you find them?

der Mast

der Schornstein

die Möve

die Kommando-
brücke

der Aufenthalts-
raum

die Rettungsboote*

der Liegestuhl

die Reling

der Küchenchef

der Kellner

die Küche

der Speisesaal

das Heck

die Treppe

die Bullaugen*

das Steuerruder

das Badezimmer

die Dusche

die Schiffsschraube

die Leiter

r Maschinist

Wachtmeister Verb hat einen schweren Tag
Sergeant Verb has a busy day

schlafen

Verb liegt im Bett und schläft.
Verb sleeps in bed.

aufwachen

Er wacht auf
He wakes up

steigen

und steigt aus dem Bett.
and climbs out of bed.

aufdrehen

Er dreht die Wasserkräne auf,
He turns on the taps,

waschen

wäscht sich die Hände
washes his hands

reiben

und reibt sein Gesicht trocken.
and rubs his face.

putzen

Er putzt sich die Zähne,
He cleans his teeth,

ausziehen

zieht seinen Schlafanzug aus,
takes off his pyjamas,

anziehen

zieht seine Kleidung an
puts on his clothes

bürsten

und bürstet sich das Haar.
and brushes his hair.

rutschen

Verb rutscht das Geländer hinunter
Verb slides down the banisters

essen

und ißt dann sein Frühstück.
and then eats his breakfast.

trinken

Er trinkt seinen Kaffee,
He drinks his coffee,

lesen

liest die Zeitung
reads the newspaper

fallen lassen

und läßt einen Teller fallen.
and drops a plate.

füttern

Er füttert den Kanarienvogel,
He feeds the canary,

schließen

schließt das Fenster
closes the window

öffnen

und öffnet die Tür.
and opens the door.

fahren

Er fährt mit seinem Wagen,
He drives his car,

gehen

geht ins Büro
walks into his office

schreiben

und schreibt einen Brief.
and writes a letter.

sprechen

Er spricht am Telefon,
He talks on the telephone,

erzählen

erzählt Nomen von einem Raubüberfall
tells Noun about a robbery

laufen

und läuft hinaus zu seinem Wagen.
and runs out to his car.

schauen

Er schaut sich ein Fenster an,
He looks at a window,

sehen

sieht einen Fußstapfen
sees a footprint

suchen

und sucht den Einbrecher.
and searches for the burglar.

verfolgen

Verb verfolgt den Einbrecher,
Verb chases the burglar,

fangen

fängt ihn
catches him

in ein Handgemenge geraten

und sie geraten in ein Handgemenge.
and they fight.

treten

Der Einbrecher tritt Verb,
The burglar kicks Verb,

schlagen

Verb schlägt den Einbrecher,
Verb hits the burglar

fallen

und er fällt um.
and he falls down.

aufheben

Verb hebt ihn auf,
Verb picks him up,

nehmen

nimmt ihn zur Polizeiwache
takes him to the police station

einsperren

und sperrt ihn ein.
and locks him in.

Inspektor Nomen und der preisgekrönte Bulle

Inspector Noun and the prize bull

Drei dumme Diebe versuchen, einen preisgekrönten Bullen zu stehlen.
Durch welche Tore geht Inspektor Nomen, um sie zu ertappen?

Three silly robbers try to steal a prize bull. Which gates does Inspector Noun go through to catch them?

das Bauernhaus

die Scheune

die Vogelscheuche

das Heu

der Garten

die Baumstämme*

der Karren

Inspektor Nomen

der Bauer

die Bäuerin

die Schweine*

der Hahn

die Puter*

der Schweinestal

der Hühnerstall

die Ferkel*

die Hühner*

die Gänschen*

die Küken*

die Gänse*

der Landarbeiter

die Enten*

der Teich

das Stroh

die Entchen*

der Stall

die Schafe*

die Lämmer*

die Ziege

10

der Schuppen

der Obstgarten

der Anhänger

der Traktor

der Pflug

der Silo

der Aufzug

der Wassertrog

das Gehege

der Schäfer

die Kühe*

der Kuhstall

der Schäferhund

die Kälber*

der Esel

der Bulle

die Pferde*

das Fohlen

der Lastwagen

Inspektor Nomen und die Fabrikspione
Inspector Noun and the factory spies

die Fabrik

Nomen steht draußen vor einer Fabrik Wache. Er sieht, wie zwei Spione herauslaufen.
Noun is on watch outside a factory. He sees two spies run out.

die Straße

Er folgt ihnen die Straße hinunter,
He follows them down the street,

das Tor

durch das Tor hindurch
through the gates

der Park

und in den Park hinein.
and into the park.

der See

Er läuft an dem See,
He walks past the lake,

die Schaukeln*

an den Schaukeln
the swings

die Marschkapelle

und an der Marschkapelle vorbei.
and the band.

die Schule

Die Spione sind bei einer Schule.
The spies are near a school.

das Gitter

Nomen blickt durch das Gitter
Noun looks through some railings

der Schulhof

und sieht sie auf dem Schulhof.
and sees them in the playground.

die Kirche

Er verfolgt sie an der Kirche vorbei,
He chases them past the church,

das Kino

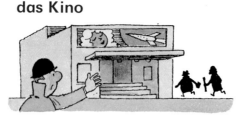

um das Kino herum
round the cinema

das Hotel

und in das Hotel hinein.
and into a hotel.

das Café

Er findet die Spione in einem Café.
He finds the spies at a café.

die Ampel

Dann gehen sie zu der Ampel
Off they go to the traffic lights

der Fußgängerübergang

und überqueren die Straße an dem Fußgängerübergang.
and walk across the crossing.

die Bushaltestelle

Sie warten an einer Bushaltestelle.
They wait at a bus stop.

der Laternenpfahl

Nomen läuft hinter einen Laternenpfahl und versteckt sich hinter einer
Noun runs round a street lamp

die Statue

and hides behind a statue.   Statue.

der Bus

Die Spione verpassen den Bus
The spies miss the bus

das Krankenhaus

und gehen zu Fuß weiter an dem Krankenhaus
and walk on past the hospital

das Loch

und an einem Loch in der
and a hole in the road.   Straße vorbei.

der Preßlufthammer

Sie sehen dem Mann mit einem Preßlufthammer zu,
They watch the man with a drill,

der Bagger

werfen einen Blick auf einen Bagger
look at a digger

die Walze

und eine Walze.
and a roller.

die Röhren*

Sie springen über einige Röhren
They jump over some pipes

die Ziegelsteine*

und Ziegelsteine.
and some bricks.

der Polizist

Da sehen sie Nomen mit einem Polizisten.
Then they see Noun with a policeman.

das Büro

Sie rennen in ein Büro,
They hurry into an office,

das Treppenhaus

das Treppenhaus hinauf
up the stairs

die Feuerleiter

und auf die Feuerleiter.
and on to the fire escape.

das Dach

Nomen verfolgt sie bis auf das Dach,
Noun chases them on to the roof,

der Fahnenmast

um einen Fahnenmast herum
round a flag pole

der Schornstein

und erwischt sie schließlich bei
and at last traps them by a chimney.   einem Schornstein.

Inspektor Nomen fliegt mit einer Düsenmaschine
Inspector Noun goes flying

Inspektor Nomen fährt zum Flughafen. Er ist auf der Suche nach einem Schmuggler.
Inspector Noun drives to the airport. He is looking for a smuggler.

die Flugkarte

Er zeigt seine Flugkarte vor.
His ticket is checked.

der Zoll

Er geht durch den Zoll
He goes through the customs

der Pass

und läßt seinen Paß abstempeln.
and has his passport stamped.

die Abflughalle

Er wartet in die Abflughalle.
He waits in the departure lounge.

die Karte

Er bekommt seine Bordkarte.
He is given his boarding pass.

die Passagiere*

Er sieht sich die anderen Passagiere an.
He looks at the other passengers.

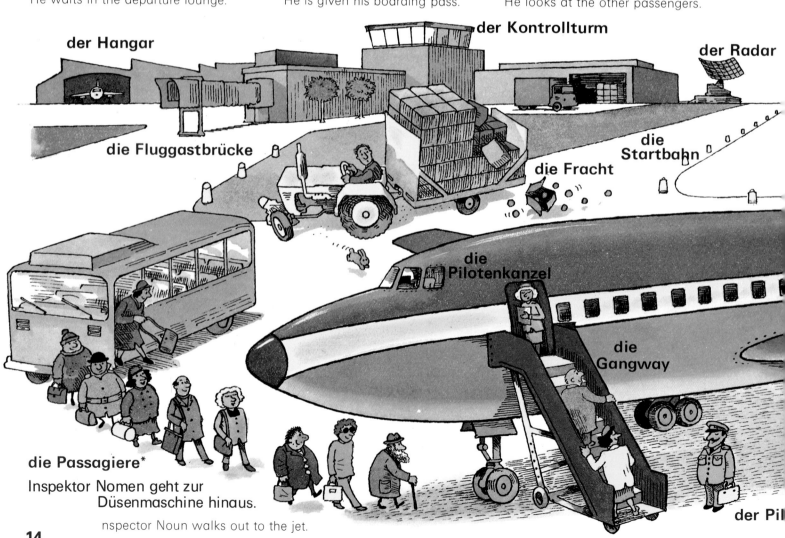

der Hangar

der Kontrollturm

der Radar

die Fluggastbrücke

die Startbahn

die Fracht

die Pilotenkanzel

die Gangway

die Passagiere*

Inspektor Nomen geht zur Düsenmaschine hinaus.
nspector Noun walks out to the jet.

der Pil

das Flugzeug

Er geht durch das Flugzeug
He walks down the plane

der Sitz

bis zu seinem Sitz.
and finds his seat.

der Sicherheitsgurt

Er befestigt seinen Sicherheitsgurt.
He fastens his safety belt.

die Startbahn

Die Düsenmaschine rollt über die Startbahn und erhebt sich in die Luft.
The jet speeds down the runway

die Luft

and takes off into the air.

die Pilotenkanzel

Nomen geht in die Pilotenkanzel.
Noun goes to the flight deck.

der Pilot

Er spricht mit dem Piloten,
He talks to the pilot,

das Instrumentenbrett

wirft einen Blick auf das Instrumentenbrett
looks at the controls

der Gang

und geht wieder zurück den Gang entlang.
and walks down the gangway.

die Goldbarren*

Er sieht die Goldbarren,
He sees the gold bars,

die Stewardess

daraufhin flüstert er der Stewardess etwas ins Ohr
so he whispers to the stewardess

der Schmuggler

und verhaftet den Schmuggler.
and arrests the smuggler.

das Heck

der Tankwagen

die Tragfläche

das Düsentriebwerk

der Gepäckwagen

das Fahrgestell

die Stewardess

der Koffer

Inspektor Nomen und der Kostümverleih
Inspector Noun and the disguise shop

Nomen und sein Assistent gehen zu einem Kostümverleih. Wieviele Kostüme probieren sie an?
Noun and his assistant go to a disguise shop. How many disguises do they try on?

die Stiefel*

die Schuhe*

die Pantoffeln*

die Hüte*

die Kappen*

die Socken*

die Schlipse*

die Hosen*

die Hemden*

die Jeans*

die Kilts*

die Handschuhe*

die Mäntel*

die Pullover*

die Anoraks*

die Latzhosen*

die Anzüge*

die Regenmäntel*

die Perücken*

die falschen Nasen*

die Schlafanzüge*

die Uniformen*

die Bärte

die Schnurrbärte*

die Shorts*

die T-shirts*

die Morgenmäntel*

die Stiefel*

die Schuhe*

die Hüte*

die Handschuhe*

die Pantoffeln*

die Röcke*

die Kleider*

die Blusen*

die Handtaschen*

die Mäntel*

die Strumpfhosen*

die Strickjacken*

die Umhänge*

die Nachthemden*

die Morgenmäntel*

die Schals*

die Taschentücher*

die Sonnenbrillen*

die Pelzmäntel*

die Perücken*

das Make-up

der Schmuck

die Uniformen*

die
Einkaufstaschen*

die Schürzen*

17

Inspektor Nomen und die Supermarktbande
Inspector Noun and the supermarket gang

Nomen geht zum Supermarkt. Er ist auf der Suche nach Lebensmitteldieben.
Noun goes to the supermarket. He is looking for some food robbers.

das Brot

Er geht am Brot
He walks past the bread

die Butter

und an der Butter vorbei
and the butter

der Käse

und sieht sich den Käse an.
and looks at the cheese.

die Milch

Er geht an der Milch
He goes past the milk

der Joghurt

und am Joghurt vorbei
and the yoghurt

die Eier*

und läßt einige Eier fallen.
and drops some eggs.

der Schinken

Er sieht sich den Schinken
Noun looks at the ham

der Speck

und den Speck an
and the bacon

der Fisch

und kriecht am Fisch vorbei.
and crawls past the fish.

das Mehl

Er blickt hinter das Mehl
He peers round the flour

der Zucker

und den Zucker
and the sugar

die Schokolade

und die Schokolade.
and the chocolate.

der Honig

Er steht beim Honig,
He stands by the honey,

die Marmelade

schaut sich die Marmelade an
looks at the jam

die Süßigkeiten*

und sucht sich ein paar Süßigkeiten aus
and chooses some sweets.

die Kuchen*

Er läuft an den Kuchen
He runs past the cakes

die Plätzchen*

und Plätzchen vorbei
and the biscuits

die Brötchen*

und macht einen großen Schritt über die Brötchen.
and steps over the bread rolls.

die Dosen*

Er stößt Dosen
He knocks over tins

die Flaschen*

und Flaschen
and bottles

die Gläser*

und Gläser um.
and jars.

die Gefriertruhe

Er ruht sich bei der Gefriertruhe aus,
He rests by the freezer,

der Korb

tritt mit dem Fuß gegen einen Korb
kicks over a basket

die Kartons*

und einige Kartons.
and some boxes.

das Fleisch

Nomen findet etwas Fleisch,
Noun finds some meat,

das Hühnchen

ein Hühnchen
a chicken

die Würstchen*

und mehrere Würstchen.
and some sausages.

die Kasse

Er läuft an den Kassen vorbei,
He runs past the cash desk,

die Einkaufstaschen*

springt über ein paar Einkaufstaschen
jumps over some bags

die Säcke*

und über einige Säcke.
and some sacks.

die Diebe*

Dann erwischt er die Diebe.
Then he catches the robbers.

der Einkaufswagen

Er lädt sie in einen Einkaufswagen
He puts them in a trolley

das Hundegefängnis

und bringt sie ins Hundegefängnis.
and takes them to the dog prison.

Detektiv Präposition und das Gespensterschloß
Detective Preposition and the haunted castle

Detektiv Präposition geht zu dem Schloß. Dort haben Gauner einen Schatz versteckt.
Detective Preposition goes to the castle. Crooks have hidden some treasure there.

an

Er kommt am Wassergraben an,
He arrives at the moat,

über

geht über die Zugbrücke
walks over the drawbridge

unter

und unter dem Torbogen hindurch.
and goes under the gatehouse.

unter

Er schaut unter einen Stein,
He looks under a stone,

mit

sucht mit seiner Taschenlampe nach dem Schatz
searches for the treasure with his torch

zwischen

und leuchtet zwischen zwei Kanonen.
and shines it between two cannons.

bei

Als er bei einer Säule stehen bleibt,
As he stops near a pillar,

in der Nähe

hört er Schritte in der Nähe
he hears the sound of footsteps

in

und schaut in einen Raum.
and looks into a room.

hinter

Ein Gespenst erscheint hinter ihm,
A ghost appears behind him

vor

und dann steht es vor ihm.
and then stands in front of him.

auf . . . zu

Er läuft auf die Treppe zu.
He runs towards the stairs.

hinunter

Er springt schnell hinunter,
He jumps quickly down,

durch

fällt durch den Fußboden,
falls through the floor

auf

landet jedoch auf seinen Füßen.
but lands on his feet.

Detektiv Pronomen kommt zur Hilfe
Detective Pronoun to the rescue

Als Präposition nicht zurückkommt, fährt Detektiv Pronomen zu dem Gespensterschloß.
When Preposition does not come back, Detective Pronoun goes to the haunted castle.

sie

Sie geht durch das Tor,
She walks through the gate,

du

ruft „Wo bist du?"
shouts "Where are you?"

ihn

und sucht ihn.
and looks for him.

er

Dann sieht sie, daß er in das Verließ gefallen ist.
Then she sees he is in the dungeon.

mir

„Hilf mir bitte," sagt er.
"Please help me," he says.

ich

„Ich zieh' dich heraus," sagt sie.
"I will pull you out," she says.

wir

„Schnell, wir müssen uns verstecken.
"Quick, we must hide.

sie

Sie kommen hier herunter
They are coming down here

uns

und werden uns sehen."
and will see us."

ihn

„Wir haben ihn gefunden," sagen die Gauner.
"We have found it," say the crooks.

sie

Plötzlich sehen die Gauner sie,
Suddenly the crooks see her

sie

aber Pronomen verhaftet sie.
but Pronoun arrests them.

Eines Nachts schlichen zehn Spione in ein Hotel, um einen berühmten Wissenschaftler zu entführen.
One night ten spies crept into a hotel to kidnap a famous scientist.

das Baby
die Decke
das Kinderbett
der Frisiertisch
der Staub-sauger
der Korri...

der Balkon
das Bett
der Kleiderschrank
das Badezimmer
die Seife
das Handtuch
der Trepp... absatz

die Lampe
der Heizkörper
das Bild
die Vorhänge*
der Tisch
der Speisesaal
die Blumen*
der Stuhl
der Lift
der Teppich
der Kinderwagen

die Küche
die Töpfe*
die Backöfen
der Spülstein
die Schürze
die Geschirrspül-maschine
die Wasch-maschine
das Treppenha...
der Kühlschrank
der Kochherd
die Bratpfanne

Als sie Inspektor Nomen kommen hörten, versteckten sie sich. Kannst du sie alle finden?
When they heard Inspector Noun coming, they hid. Can you find them all?

Inspektor Nomen verfolgt die Gauner
Inspector Noun chases the crooks

das Gefängnis

Zwei Gauner entkommen aus dem Gefängnis. Nomen läuft hinter ihnen her.
Two crooks escape from prison. Noun runs after them.

das Tandem

Sie fahren auf einem Tandem davon.
They ride away on a tandem.

das Fahrrad

Nomen verfolgt sie auf einem Fahrrad.
Noun chases them on a bicycle.

der Roller

Sie springen auf einen Roller.
They jump on a scooter.

die Rollschuhe*

Nomen folgt ihnen auf Rollschuhen.
Noun follows them on roller skates.

das Auto

Die Gauner stehlen ein Auto.
The crooks steal a car.

das Taxi

Nomen hält ein Taxi an.
Noun hires a taxi.

der Lastwagen

Sie entkommen in einem Lastwagen.
They drive off in a lorry.

der Lieferwagen

Nomen fährt mit einem Lieferwagen hinter ihnen her.
Noun follows them in a van.

das Flugzeug

Die Gauner heben in einem Flugzeug ab.
The crooks fly off in a plane.

der Hubschrauber

Nomen verfolgt sie in einem Hubschrauber.
Noun chases them in a helicopter.

der Fallschirm

Sie schweben an einem Fallschirm herab.
They come down by parachute.

der Zug

Sie steigen in einen Zug.
They catch a train.

das Motorboot

Sie stehlen ein Motorboot.
They steal a motor boat.

das Ruderboot

Sie springen in ein Ruderboot.
They jump into a rowing boat.

der Pferdetransporter

Sie stehlen einen Pferdetransporter.
They steal a horse box.

das Motorrad

Sie haben einen Unfall auf einem Motorrad.
They crash a motorbike.

der Ballon

Nomen landet in einem Ballon.
Noun lands in a balloon.

der Rennwagen

Nomen jagt sie in einem Rennwagen.
Noun drives after them in a racing car.

das Segelboot

Nomen folgt ihnen in einem Segelboot.
Noun follows in a sailing boat.

das Kanu

Nomen paddelt in einem Kanu hinter ihnen her.
Noun paddles after them in a canoe.

die Feuerwehr

Nomen wird von einer Feuerwehr mitgenommen.
Noun has a lift on a fire engine.

der Krankenwagen

Nomen fängt sie und transportiert sie in einem
Noun catches them and takes them away in an ambulance.   Krankenwagen ab.

Die Schule für Verbdetektive

School for Verb Detectives

Hier sehen wir viele Verben in einer Schule für Detektive.
Kannst du die sechs Gauner entdecken, die sie beobachten?

Here are lots of Verbs at a school for detectives.
Can you find the six crooks watching them?

schieben

marschieren

ins Wasser springen

springen

schwimmen

Ball spielen

tragen

ringen

graben

schießen

kriechen

Seilchen springen

sich verstecken

lächeln

finden

ziehen

lachen

sitzen

werfen

reiten

rudern

Schlittschuh laufen

fliegen

pusten

bauen

schneiden

um die Wette laufen

stehen

malen

singen

ein Instrument spielen

dirigieren

warten

denken

schaukeln

tanzen

hüpfen

kochen

stricken

basteln

nähen

anhalten

Detektiv Adverb und der Fleischdieb
Detective Adverb and the meat thief

der Metzger

der Bäcker

die Blumen*

Eines Abends beobachtete Detektiv Adverb, wie ein Mann Fleisch stahl. Er sah folgendes.
One evening Detective Adverb saw a man stealing some meat. This is what he saw.

langsam

Ein Hund lief langsam daher
A dog was walking slowly along,

laut

und schnüffelte laut nach Essen.
sniffing loudly for food.

traurig

Dann setzte er sich traurig hin.
Then he sat down sadly.

plötzlich

bald

glücklich

Plötzlich stahl ein Mann etwas Fleisch, und der Hund hatte es bald aufgefressen. Er wackelte glücklich mit
A man suddenly grabbed some meat   and the dog soon ate it.   He wagged his tail happily.   dem Schwanz.

liebevoll

Der Mann streichelte den Hund liebevoll.
The man gently patted the dog

wütend

Der Metzger schimpfte wütend,
The butcher shouted angrily

schnell

und der Mann lief schnell davon.
and the man ran quickly away.

wild

Der Hund bellte wie wild.
The dog barked fiercely.

fast

Der Metzger erwischte ihn fast,
The butcher almost caught it

ebenfalls

aber er lief ebenfalls davon.
but it also ran away.

Detektiv Adjektivs Bericht
Detective Adjective's Report

Detektiv Adjektiv sah den Hund und den Mann. Sie beschreibt sie folgendermaßen:
Detective Adjective saw the dog and the man. This is her description of them.

dünn

Der Hund hatte einen dünnen Kopf,
The dog had a thin head,

spitz

spitze Ohren
pointed ears

braun

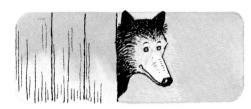

und braune Augen.
and brown eyes.

schwarz

Er hatte ein schwarzes Fell,
It had a black coat,

lang

einen langen Schwanz
a long tail

rot

und ein rotes Halsband.
and a red collar.

rund

Der Mann hatte ein rundes Gesicht,
The man had a round face,

lockig

lockige Haare
curly hair

grau

und einen grauen Bart.
and a grey beard.

grün

Er trug einen grünen Hut,
He wore a green hat,

alt

einen alten Mantel
an old coat

weiß

und ein weißes Hemd.
and a white shirt.

blau

Er trug eine blaue Hose,
He had blue trousers,

gelb

gelbe Socken
yellow socks

groß

und große Stiefel.
and big boots.

Inspektor Nomen und die Schmuggler
Inspector Noun and the smugglers

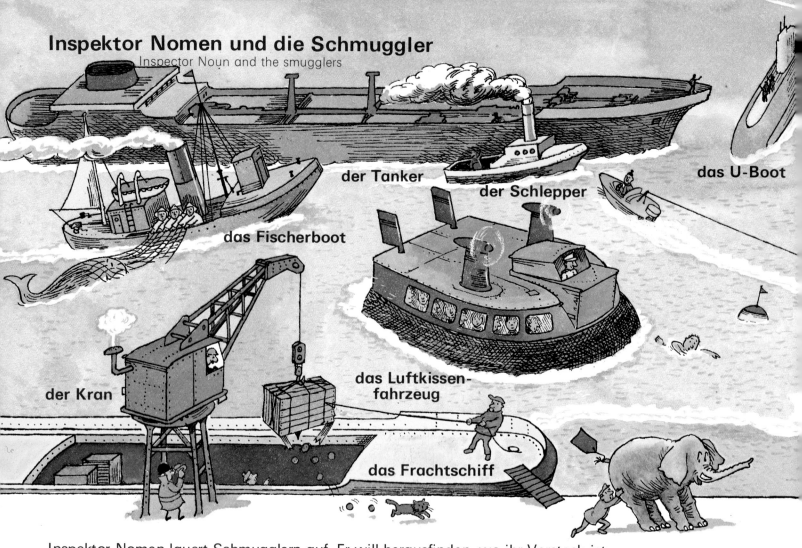

der Tanker

der Schlepper

das U-Boot

das Fischerboot

der Kran

das Luftkissen-
fahrzeug

das Frachtschiff

Inspektor Nomen lauert Schmugglern auf. Er will herausfinden, wo ihr Versteck ist.
Inspector Noun is waiting for some smugglers. He wants to find their hide-out.

das Motorboot

Er sieht ein Motorboot
He sees a motor boat

die Schmuggler*

und beobachtet die Schmuggler.
and watches the smugglers.

der Strand

Er folgt ihnen den Strand entlang.
He follows them along the beach.

die Sandburg

Sie gehen an einer Sandburg vorbei,
They walk past a sandcastle,

der Eimer

treten gegen einen Eimer
kick over a bucket

der Sonnenschirm

und stoßen einen Sonnenschirm um
and knock down an umbrella.

der Spaten

Einer tritt auf einen Spaten,
One steps on a spade,

der Ball

ein anderer gegen einen Ball.
another kicks a ball.

das Picknick

Die Schmuggler legen eine
The smugglers stop for a picnic. Picknickspause ein.

das Wrack

die Hafenmauer

das Tragflächenboot

der Wasserskiläufer

die Autofähre

die Boje

die Kisten*

das Lagerhaus

die Kieselsteine*

Nomen sitzt auf den Kieselsteinen.
Noun sits on the pebbles.

der Krebs

Er hebt einen Krebs auf
He picks up a crab

der Felsentümpel

und setzt ihn in einen Felsentümpel.
and puts it into a rock pool.

die Felsen*

Er folgt den Männern bis zu den Felsen,
He follows the men to the rocks,

der Seetang

rutscht auf etwas Seetang aus
slips on some seaweed

der Leuchtturm

und erreicht den Leuchtturm.
and reaches the lighthouse.

die Klippe

Er klettert auf die Klippe,
He climbs up the cliff,

der Tunnel

kriecht in einen Tunnel
crawls into a tunnel

die Höhle

und findet das Versteck der Schmuggler in einer Höhle.
and finds the smugglers' hide-out in a cave.

Inspektor Nomen in Gefahr
Inspector Noun in danger

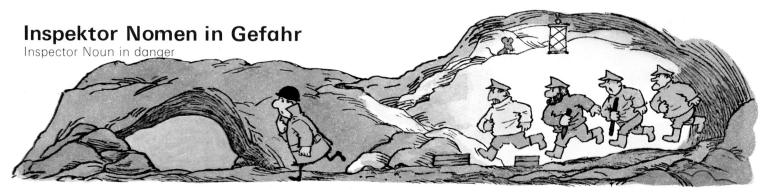

Nomen findet die Schmuggler in ihrer Höhle. Aber sie bemerken, daß er allein ist und machen sich daran,
Noun finds the smugglers in their cave. But they see he is alone and start to chase him.   ihn zu verfolgen.

die Straße

Er rennt weg eine Straße hinunter,
He runs away along a road,

die Brücke

überquert eine Brücke
crosses over a bridge

die Kreuzung

und erreicht eine Kreuzung.
and reaches a crossroads.

der Wegweiser

Nomen bleibt stehen, um einen Wegweiser zu lesen,
Noun stops to read a sign post,

der Pfad

läuft weiter einen Pfad hinab
runs on down a path

die Hecke

und kriecht durch eine
and crawls through a hedge.   Hecke.

die Bäume*

Er läuft auf ein paar Bäume zu.
He runs towards some trees.

der Fluß

Dann kommt er an einen Fluß
Then he comes to a river

das Floß

und paddelt auf einem Floß zum
and paddles across on a raft.   anderen Ufer.

der Wasserfall

Mit Mühe rettet er sich vor einem Wasserfall,
He just misses a waterfall,

der Hügel

eilt einen Hügel hinauf
hurries up a hill

der Zaun

und springt über einen Zaun.
and jumps over a fence.

der Kanal

Nomen bleibt an einem Kanal stehen,
Noun stops by a canal,

der Kahn

springt auf einen Kahn
leaps on to a barge

die Schleuse

und steigt an einer Schleuse wieder ab.
and jumps off again at a lock.

das Tor

Nomen klettert über ein Tor,
Noun climbs over a gate,

die Zelte*

rennt an ein paar Zelten vorbei
hurries past some tents

die Leine

und stolpert über eine Leine.
and trips over a rope.

der Wohnwagen

Er rennt weiter an einem Wohnwagen vorbei,
He runs past a caravan,

der Bach

erreicht einen Bach
reaches a stream

die Steine*

und balanciert über die Steine ans andere Ufer.
and crosses over by the stepping stones.

die Staumauer

Er eilt über eine Staumauer,
He dashes across a dam,

die Windmühle

an einer Windmühle vorbei
past a windmill

der Wald

und in einen Wald hinein.
and into a forest.

der Berg

Er klettert auf einen Berg,
He starts to climb a mountain,

die Seilbahn

fährt mit einer Seilbahn
then rides in a cable car

der Schnee

und tritt hinaus in den Schnee
and steps out into snow.

die Schier*

Er probiert ein Paar Schier an,
He tries on some skis,

der Schlitten

rodelt auf einem Schlitten den Hang hinunter
slides down on a toboggan

die Mauer

und klettert über eine Mauer.
and then climbs over a wall.

der Raum

Er läuft in einen dunklen Raum
Noun runs into a dark room

das Licht

und knipst das Licht an.
and switches on the light.

die Polizeiwache

Die Schmuggler sind ihm auf einer Polizeiwache in die Falle gegangen.
The smugglers are caught in a police station.

Inspektor Nomen im Zoo

Inspector Noun at the zoo

Im Zoo ist der Löwe aus seinem Käfig ausgebrochen. Welchem Pfad folgt Nomen, um ihn zu finden?

At the zoo the lion has escaped from its cage. Which path does Noun go along to find it?

der Käfig

der Wärter

Inspektor Nomen

der Eisbär

die Schlangen*

der Elefant

das Kamel

die Seehunde*

das Kängeruh

der Tiger

die Giraffe

die Pinguine*

die Strauße*

die Eule

die Flamingos*

die Krokodile*

die Nilpferde*

die Nashörner*

der Löwe

das Zebra

der Büffel

das Rentier

der Panda

die Ziegen*

die Bären*

das Stachelschwein

der Pelikan

der Biber

der Papagei

der Tukan

die Affen*

die Schildkröte

der Wolf

der Adler

35

Inspektor Nomen sucht nach Anhaltspunkten

Inspector Noun looks for clues

Nomen öffnet die Tür zu seinem Büro. „Hier war jemand," denkt er und macht sich auf
die Suche nach Anhaltspunkten.

Noun opens the door of his office. "Someone has been in here," he thinks and looks for clues.

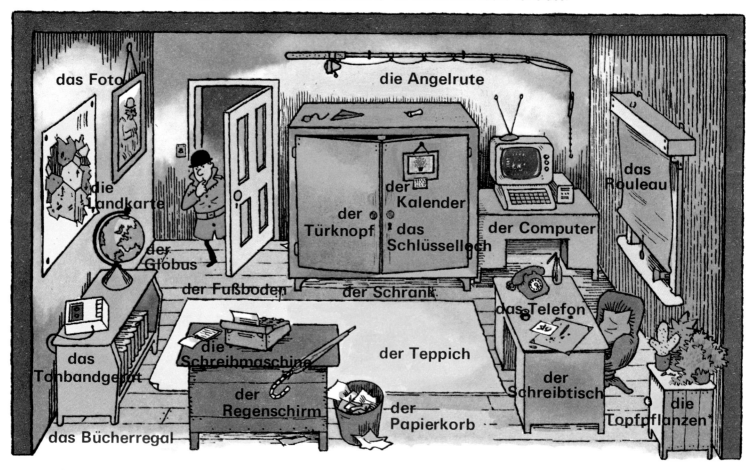

das Foto

die Angelrute

die Landkarte

der Globus

der Türknopf

der Kalender

das Schlüsselloch

der Computer

das Rouleau

der Fußboden

der Schrank

das Telefon

das Tonbandgerät

die Schreibmaschine

der Teppich

der Schreibtisch

der Regenschirm

der Papierkorb

die Topfpflanzen

das Bücherregal

der Fußboden

Er betrachtet den Fußboden,
He looks at the floor,

die Schublade

entdeckt eine offene Schublade
finds an open drawer

die Armbanduhr

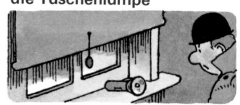

und hebt eine Armbanduhr auf.
and picks up a watch.

der Schlüssel

Er findet einen Schlüssel
He finds a key

das Taschentuch

und ein Taschentuch
and a handkerchief

die Taschenlampe

und eine Taschenlampe.
and a torch.

der Füllfederhalter

die Briefmarke

der Briefumschlag

Irgendjemand hat seinen Füllfederhalter benutzt, eine Briefmarke gestohlen und einen Briefumschlag geöffnet.
Someone has used his pen,   stolen a stamp   and opened an envelope.

das Notizbuch

Jemand hat sein Notizbuch gelesen,
Someone has read his notebook,

der Computer

mit seinem Computer gespielt
played with his computer

der Taschenrechner

und seinen Taschenrechner fallen
and dropped his calculator. **lassen.**

der Bleistift

Jemand hat seinen Bleistift durchgebrochen,
Someone has broken his pencil,

das Getränk

sein Getränk ausgetrunken
finished his drink

das Butterbrot

und in sein Butterbrot gebissen.
and eaten his sandwich.

der Hammer
der Pinsel
die Säge
der Schraubenzieher

die Untertassen*
die Teller*
die Tassen*
die Streichhölzer*
die Messer*
die Gabeln*
die Löffel*
die Gläser*
die Pfeife
der Krug
der Verbandskasten
die Sicherheitsnadeln*
die Verbände*
der Schallplattenspieler
die Schallplatten*

die Lupe
der Feldstecher
der Fotoapparat
die Handschellen*
der Bindfaden
die Farbe
der Wecker
die Nägel*
das Geld
die Papiere*
die Bücher*

die Schere
das Taschenmesser
das Schwert
die Axt

Dann sieht er in seinen Schrank und findet den Einbrecher.
Then he looks in his cupboard and finds the burglar.

Inspektor Nomen fängt einen Weltraumspion

Inspector Noun catches a space spy

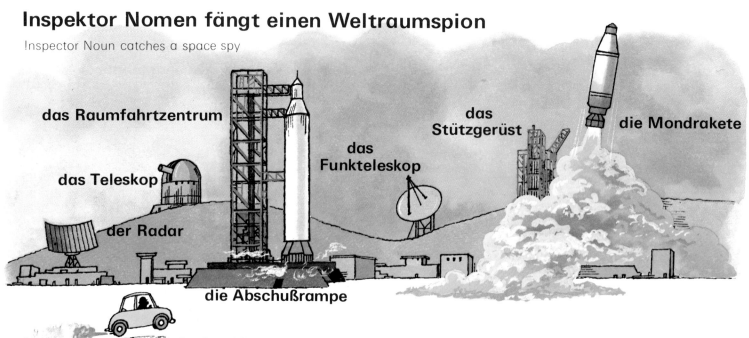

das Raumfahrtzentrum

das Teleskop

der Radar

das Funkteleskop

das Stützgerüst

die Mondrakete

die Abschußrampe

Nomen kommt gerade in dem Moment am Raumfahrtzentrum an, als eine Rakete abgeschossen wird.
Er weiß, daß ein Spion an Bord ist.

Noun reaches the space launch station just as a rocket blasts off. He knows there is a spy on board.

der Raumanzug

Er zieht einen Raumanzug an
He puts on a space suit,

die Astronauten*

und trifft zwei Astronauten,
meets two astronauts

die Abschußrampe

die ihn zur Abschußrampe bringen.
and is taken to the launch pad.

das Raumschiff

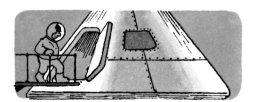

Er steigt in das Raumschiff,
He goes into the space craft,

die Liege

legt sich auf eine Liege,
lies on a couch

die Rakete

und die Rakete hebt ab.
and the rocket takes off.

die Erde

Er sieht die Erde unter sich
He sees the earth below

die Sonne

und blickt auf die Sonne
and looks at the sun

die Sterne*

und die Sterne.
and the stars.

die Raumfähre

Er schießt an einer Raumfähre,
He whizzes past a space shuttle,

der Satellit

einem Satelliten
a satellite

die Raumstation

und einer Raumstation vorbei.
and a space station.

das Mondfahrzeug

die
Mondlandefähre

Nomen landet auf dem Mond. Die andere Rakete ist schon da.
Noun lands on the moon. The other rocket is there.

das Mondfahrzeug

Er fährt mit einem Mondfahrzeug,
He rides on a moon buggy, sees footprints in the moon dust and catches the spy by a moon rock.

der Mondstaub

bemerkt Fußstapfen im Mondstaub

das Mondgestein

und fängt den Spion hinter einem
Brocken Mondgestein.

der Weltraum

Er fliegt zurück in den Weltraum.
He takes off into space again.

der Meteor

Ein Meteor trifft die Raumkapsel.
The module is hit by a meteor.

der Spaziergang im All

Nomen macht einen Spaziergang im All.
Noun goes for a space walk.

die Antenne

Er repariert die Antenne.
He mends an antenna.

die Erdumlaufbahn

Die Raumkapsel kehrt in die Erdumlaufbahn zurück
The module goes into orbit

das Meer

und landet im Meer.
and they splash down in the sea.

die Einstiegsluke

Sie klettern aus der Einstiegsluke.
They climb out of the nose cone.

die Froschmänner*

Froschmänner stehen bereit, um ihnen zu helfen.
Frogmen are there to help them. The mission is safely over.

die Mission

Die Mission ist zu einem
sicheren Ende gekommen.

INDEX

On this page is the start of the alphabetical list of all the single words on the pictures in this book. The German word comes first, then there is its pronunication in *italics*, followed by the English translation.

Although some German words look like English ones, they are not pronounced in the same way. And some letters have different sounds. In German, *w* sounds like English *v*, *v* sounds like *f*, *z* like *ts*, and *j* like *y* in young. There are also some sounds in German which are quite unlike sounds in English.

The pronunciation is a guide to help you say the words correctly. They may look funny or strange. Just read them as if they are English words, except for these special rules:

ah	— is said like *s* in *farther*
a	— is said like *ah* but shorter
ow	— is like *ow* in cow
ew	— is different from any sound in English. To make it say *ee* with your lips rounded
ee	— is like *ee* in *week*
ay	— is like *ay* in *day*
y	— is like *y* in *try*, except when it comes before a vowel. Then it sounds like *y* in *young*
g	— as *g* in *garden*
ch	— is said like *ch* in the Scottish word *loch*
kh	— is said like the *h* in *huge*
r	— is made at the back of your mouth and sounds a little like gargling
e(r)	— is like the *e* in the (not *thee*). When the *r* is in brackets *(r)*, it is not said
u(r)	— is like *i* in *bird*. The *r* is not said
oo	— is a short vowel, like in *foot*
o͞o	— is a long vowel, like in *food*

40

German	Pronunciation	English
der Briefumschlag	derr breef-oom-shlahk	envelope
das Brot	dass broat	bread
die Brücke	dee brewke(r)	bridge
die Bücher	dee bewkher	books
das Bücherregal	dass bewkher-raygal	bookcase
der Büffel	derr bewfel	buffalo
der Bug	derr book	bow (of ship)
die Bullaugen	dee bool-owgen	port holes
der Bulle	derr boole(r)	bull
das Büro	dass bewro	office
bürsten	bewrsten	to brush
der Bus	derr booss	bus
die Bushaltestelle	dee boos-halte(r)-shtelle(r)	bus stop
die Butter	dee booter	butter
das Butterbrot	dass booter-broat	sandwich
das Café	dass kafay	café
der Computer	derr komputer	computer
das Dach	dass dach	roof
das Deck	dass dek	deck
die Decke	dee deke(r)	blanket
denken	denken	to think
die Diamanten	dee dee-amanten	diamonds
der Dieb	derr deep	robber, thief
dirigieren	dirigeeren	to conduct
die Dosen	dee doazen	tins
du	doo	you
dünn	dewn	thin
durch	doorch	through
die Dusche	dee dooshe(r)	shower
die Düsenmaschine	dee dewzen-masheene(r)	jet
das Düsentriebwerk	dass dewzen-treep-vairk	engine
ebenfalls	ayben-falls	also
die Eier	dee eyer	eggs
der Eimer	derr eymer	bucket
die Einkaufstaschen	dee eyne-kowfs-tashen	shopping bags
der Einkaufswagen	derr eyne-kowfs-vahgen	shopping trolley
einsperren	eyne-shperren	to lock in
die Einstiegsluke	dee eyne-shteeks-looke(r)	nose cone
der Eisbär	derr eyss-bair	polar bear
der Elefant	derr elefant	elephant
der Empfang	derr empfank	reception
die Entchen	dee entkhen	ducklings
die Enten	dee enten	ducks
er	err	he
die Erbsen	dee airpsen	peas
die Erdbeeren	dee airt-bairen	strawberries
die Erde	dee airde(r)	earth
die Erdumlaufbahn	dee aird-oom-lowf-bahn	orbit
erzälen	err-tsaylen	to tell
der Esel	derr ayzel	donkey
essen	essen	to eat
die Fabrik	dee fabreek	factory
der Fahnenmast	derr fahnenmast	flag pole
fahren	fahren	to drive
das Fahrgestell	dass fahr-geshtell	wheels
das Fahrrad	dass fahr-raht	bicycle
fallen	fallen	to fall
fallen lassen	fallen lassen	to drop
das Fallreep	dass fallreep	gang plank
der Fallschirm	derr fall-sheerm	parachute
fangen	fangen	to catch
die Farbe	dee farbe(r)	paint
fast	fast	almost
der Feldstecher	derr felt-shtekher	binoculars
die Felsen	dee felzen	rocks
der Felsentümpel	derr felzen-tewmpel	rock pool
die Ferkel	dee fairkel	piglets
der Fernseher	derr fern-zayer	television
die Feuerleiter	dee foyer-lyter	fire escape
die Feuerwehr	dee foyer-vair	fire engine
finden	finden	to find
der Fisch	derr fish	fish
das Fischerboot	dass fisher-boat	fishing boat
die Flagge	dee flagge(r)	flag
die Flamingos	dee flamingoaz	flamingos
die Flaschen	dee flashen	bottles
das Fleisch	dass flysh	meat
fliegen	fleegen	to fly
das Floß	dass floass	raft
die Fluggastbrücke	dee flook-gast-brewke(r)	passenger bridge
der Flughafen	derr flook-hahfen	airport
die Flugkarte	dee flook-karte(r)	ticket
das Flugzeug	dass flook-tsoyk	plane
der Fluß	derr flooss	river
das Fohlen	dass foalen	foal
das Foto	dass foto	photograph
der Fotoapparat	derr foto-apparaht	camera
die Fracht	dee fracht	cargo
das Frachtschiff	dass fracht-shiff	cargo boat
die Frau	dee frow	woman
der Frisiertisch	derr friseer-tish	dressing table
die Froschmänner	dee frosh-menner	frogmen
der Füllfederhalter	derr-fewl-fayder-halter	pen
das Funkteleskop	dass foonk-teleskoap	radio telescope
der Fußboden	derr fooss-boaden	floor
der Fußgängerübergang	derr fooss-genger-ewber-gank	crossing
füttern	fewtern	to feed
die Gabeln	dee gahbeln	forks
der Gang	derr gank	gangway
die Gangway	dee gangway	steps
die Gänschen	dee genss-khen	goslings
die Gänse	dee genze(r)	geese
der Garten	derr garten	garden
das Gefängnis	dass gefengnis	prison
die Gefriertruhe	dee gefreertroo-e(r)	freezer
das Gehege	dass gehayge(r)	yard
gehen	gayen	to walk
gelb	gelp	yellow
das Geld	dass gelt	money
das Gemüse	dass gemewze(r)	vegetables
der Gepäckwagen	derr gepeck-vahgen	baggage train
die Geschirrspülmaschine	dass gesheer-shpewl-masheene(r)	dishwasher

German	Pronunciation	English
das Getränk	dass getrenk	a drink
die Giraffe	dee giraffe(r)	giraffe
das Gitter	dass gitter	railings
die Gläser	dee glayzer	glasses, jars
der Globus	derr gloabooss	globe
glücklich	glewk-likh	happily
die Goldbarren	dee golt-barren	gold bars
graben	grahben	to dig
grau	grow	grey
groß	groass	big
grün	grewn	green
die Hafenmauer	dee hahfen-mower	harbour wall
der Hahn	derr hahn	cockerel
die Halle	dee halle(r)	lounge
der Hammer	derr hammer	hammer
in ein Handgemenge geraten	in eyne hantgemenge(r) gerahten	to fight
die Handschellen	dee hant-shellen	handcuffs
die Handschuhe	dee hant-shoo-e(r)	gloves
die Handtaschen	dee hant-tashen	handbags
das Handtuch	dass hant-tooch	towel
der Hangar	derr hangar	hangar
das Heck	dass hek	stern, tail
die Hecke	dee heke(r)	hedge
der Heizkörper	derr hyts-ku(r)per	radiator
die Hemden	dee hemden	shirts
das Heu	dass hoy	hay
die Himbeeren	dee him-bairen	raspberries
hinter	hinter	behind
hinunter	hinoonter	down
die Höhle	dee hu(r)le(r)	cave
der Honig	derr hoanig	honey
die Hosen	dee hoazen	trousers
das Hotel	dass hotel	hotel
der Hubschrauber	derr hoop-shrowber	helicopter
der Hügel	derr hewgel	hill
das Hühnchen	dass hewn-khen	chicken
die Hühner	dee hewner	hens
der Hühnerstall	derr hewner-shtall	hen house
hüpfen	hewpfen	to hop
die Hüte	dee hewte(r)	hats
ich	ikh	I
ihn	een	he, it
ihr	eer	her, it
in	in	into
in der Nähe	in derr naye(r)	near
Inspektor Nomen	inspektor nomen	Inspector Noun
das Instrumentenbrett	dass instroomentenbrett	controls
ein Instrument spielen	eyne instrooment shpeelen	to play (an instrument)
die Jeans	dee jeans	jeans
der Joghurt	derr yogoort	yoghurt
die Jungen	dee yoongen	boys
die Kabine	dee kabeene(r)	cabin
der Käfig	derr kayfik	cage
der Kahn	derr kahn	barge
die Kälber	dee kelber	calves
der Kalender	derr kalender	calendar
das Kamel	dass kamel	camel
der Kamin	derr kameen	fireplace
der Kanal	derr kanahl	canal
das Kängeruh	dass kengooroo	kangaroo
das Kanu	dass kanoo	canoe
der Kapitän	derr kapitayn	captain
die Kappen	dee kappen	caps
der Karren	derr karren	cart
die Karte	dee karte(r)	pass
die Kartoffeln	dee kartoffeln	potatoes
die Kartons	dee kartoanz	boxes
der Käse	derr kayze(r)	cheese
die Kasse	dee kasse(r)	cash desk
der Kellner	derr kellner	waiter
die Kette	dee kette(r)	chain
die Kieselsteine	dee keezel-shtyne(r)	pebbles
die Kilts	dee kilts	kilts
das Kinderbett	dass kinderbett	cot
der Kinderwagen	derr kinder-vahgen	pram
das Kino	dass keeno	cinema
die Kirche	dee keerkhe(r)	church
die Kirschen	dee keershen	cherries
das Kissen	dass kissen	cushion
die Kisten	dee kisten	crates
die Kleider	dee klyder	dresses
der Kleiderschrank	derr klyder-shrank	wardrobe
die Klippe	dee klippe(r)	cliff
kochen	kochen	to cook
der Kochherd	derr koch-hairt	cooker
der Koffer	derr koffer	suitcase
die Kohle	dee koale(r)	coal
die Kohlköpfe	dee koal-ku(r)pfe(r)	cabbages
die Koje	dee koa-ye(r)	bunk
die Kommandobrücke	dee kommandobrewke(r)	bridge (of ship)
der Kontrollturm	derr kontrol-toorm	control tower
das Kopfkissen	dass kopf-kissen	pillow
der Korb	derr korp	basket
der Korridor	derr korridor	corridor
der Kran	derr krahn	crane
das Krankenhaus	dass kranken-howss	hospital
der Krankenwagen	derr kranken-vahgen	ambulance
der Krebs	derr kreps	crab
der Kreuzung	derr kroytsoonk	cross road
kriechen	kreekhen	to crawl
die Krokodile	dee krokodeele(r)	crocodiles
der Krug	derr krook	jug
die Küche	dee kewkhe(r)	kitchen
die Kuchen	dee koochen	cakes
der Küchenchef	derr kewkhen-shef	chef
die Kühe	dee kewe(r)	cows
der Kühlschrank	derr kewl-shrank	refrigerator
der Kuhstall	derr koo-shtall	cowshed
die Küken	dee kewken	chicks
lächeln	lekheln	to smile
lachen	lachen	to laugh
der Laderaum	derr laderowm	hold (of ship)
das Lagerhaus	dass lager-howss	warehouse
die Lämmer	dee lemmer	lambs
die Lampe	dee lampe(r)	lamp
der Landarbeiter	derr lant-arbyter	farm worker
die Landkarte	dee lant-karte(r)	map
lang	lank	long
langsam	langzam	slowly
der Lastwagen	derr last-vahgen	lorry
der Laternenpfahl	derr latairnen-pfahl	lamp post
die Latzhosen	dee lats-hoazen	dungarees

German	Pronunciation	English
der Lauch	*derr lowkh*	leek
laufen	*lowfen*	to run
laut	*lowt*	loudly
die Leine	*dee lyne(r)*	rope
die Leiter	*dee lyter*	ladder
lesen	*layzen*	to read
der Leuchtturm	*derr loykht-toorm*	lighthouse
das Licht	*dass likht*	light
liebevoll	*leebefoll*	gently
der Lieferwagen	*derr leèfer-vahgen*	van
die Liege	*dee leege(r)*	couch
der Liegestuhl	*derr leege(r)-shtool*	deckchair
der Lift	*derr lift*	lift
das Loch	*dass loch*	hole
lockig	*lokik*	curly
die Löffel	*dee lu(r)fel*	spoons
der Löwe	*derr lu(r)ve(r)*	lion
die Luft	*dee looft*	air
das Luftkissen-fahrzeug	*dass looft-kissen-fahr-tsoyk*	hovercraft
die Luke	*dee looke(r)*	hatch
die Lupe	*dee loope(r)*	magnifying glass
die Mädchen	*dee meht-khen*	girls
das Make-up	*dass 'make-up'*	make-up
malen	*mahlen*	paint
der Mann	*derr mann*	man
die Mannschafts-kabine	*dee mann-shafts-kabeene(r)*	crew's cabin
die Mäntel	*dee mentel*	coats
der Markt	*derr markt*	market
die Marmelade	*dee marmelahde(r)*	jam
marschieren	*marsheeren*	march
die Marschkapelle	*dee marsh-kapelle(r)*	band
der Maschinen-raum	*derr masheenen-rowm*	engine room
der Maschinist	*derr masheenist*	engineer
der Mast	*derr mast*	mast
der Matrose	*derr matroaze(r)*	sailor
die Mauer	*dee mower*	wall
das Meer	*dass mair*	sea
das Mehl	*dass mayl*	flour
die Melone	*dee meloane(r)*	melon
die Messer	*dee messer*	knives
der Meteor	*derr may-tee-oar*	meteor
der Metzger	*derr metsger*	butcher
die Milch	*dee milkh*	milk
mir	*meer*	me, my
die Mission	*dee miss-ee-oan*	mission
mit	*mit*	with
die Möhren	*dee muren*	carrots
das Mondfahrzeug	*dass moant-fahr-tsoyk*	moon buggy
das Mondgestein	*dass moant-geshtyne*	moon rock
die Mond-landefähre	*dee moant-landefehre(r)*	lunar module
die Mondrakete	*dee moant-rakayte(r)*	moon rocket
der Mondstaub	*derr moant-shtowp*	moon dust
die Morgenmäntel	*dee morgen-mantel*	dressing gowns
das Motorboot	*dass motoar-boat*	motor boat
das Motorrad	*dass motoar-raht*	motor bike
die Möwe	*dee mu(r)ve(r)*	gull
die Nachthemden	*dee nacht-hemden*	nightdresses
die Nägel	*dee naygel*	nails
nähen	*nayen*	to sew
die falschen Nasen	*dee falshen nahzen*	false noses
die Nashörner	*dee nahz-hurner*	rhinoceroses
nehmen	*naymen*	to take
die Nilpferde	*dee neel-pfairt*	hippo-potamuses
das Notizbuch	*dass notits-booch*	notebook
das Obst	*dass oapst*	fruit
der Obstgarten	*derr oapst-garten*	orchard
öffnen	*u(r)fnen*	to open
die Orangen	*dee oronjen*	oranges
die Pampelmuse	*dee pampelmooze(r)*	grapefruit
der Panda	*derr panda*	panda
die Pantoffeln	*dee pantoffeln*	slippers
der Papagei	*derr papagye*	parrot
die Papiere	*dee papeere(r)*	papers
der Papierkorb	*derr papeer-korp*	wastepaper basket
der Park	*derr park*	park
der Pass	*derr pass*	passport
die Passagiere	*dee passajeere(r)*	passengers
der Pelikan	*der pelikahn*	pelican
die Pelzmäntel	*dee pelts-mentel*	fur coats
die Perücken	*dee perewken*	wigs
der Pfad	*derr pfaht*	path
die Pfeife	*dee pfyfe(r)*	whistle
die Pferde	*dee pfairde(r)*	horses
der Pferde-transporter	*derr pfairde(r)-transporter*	horse box
der Pfirsich	*derr pfeerzikh*	peach
die Pflaumen	*dee pflowmen*	plums
der Pflug	*derr pflook*	plough
das Picknick	*dass piknik*	picnic
der Pilot	*derr peeloat*	pilot
die Pilotenkanzel	*dee peeloaten-kantsel*	flight deck
die Pilze	*dee piltse(r)*	mushrooms
die Pinguine	*dee pingoo-eene(r)*	penguins
der Pinsel	*derr pinzel*	brush
die Plätzchen	*dee plets-khen*	biscuits
plötzlich	*plu(r)ts-likh*	suddenly
die Polizeiwache	*dee politsye-vache(r)*	police station
der Polizist	*derr politsist*	policeman
der Preßluft-hammer	*derr press-looft-hammer*	drill
die Pullover	*dee poolover*	jerseys
pusten	*poosten*	to blow
die Puter	*dee pooter*	turkeys
putzen	*pootsen*	to clean
der Radar	*derr raydar*	radar
die Radieschen	*dee radeez-khen*	radishes
die Rakete	*dee rakayte(r)*	rocket
der Raum	*derr rowm*	room
der Raumanzug	*derr rowm-antsook*	space suit
die Raumfähre	*dee rowm-fehre(r)*	space shuttle
das Raumfahrt-zentrum	*dass rowm-fahrt-tsentroom*	space launch station
die Raumkapsel	*dee rowm-kapsel*	command module
das Raumschiff	*dass rowm-schiff*	space craft
die Raumstation	*dee rowm-shtatsee-oan*	space station
die Regale	*dee raygahle(r)*	shelves
die Regenmäntel	*dee raygen-mentel*	raincoats

German	Pronunciation	English
der Regenschirm	derr raygen-sheerm	umbrella
reiben	ryben	to rub
reiten	ryten	to ride
die Reling	dee raylink	railings
der Rennwagen	derr renn-vahgen	racing car
das Rentier	dass rehn-teer	reindeer
die Rettungsboote	dee rettoongz-boate(r)	lifeboats
ringen	ringen	to wrestle
die Röcke	dee ru(r)ke(r)	skirts
die Röhren	dee ruren	pipes
der Roller	derr roller	scooter
die Rollschuhe	dee roll-shoo-en	roller skates
der Rosenkohl	derr roazen-koal	brussel sprouts
rot	roat	red
die Rote Bete	dee roate(r) bayte(r)	beetroot
das Rouleau	dass rooloa	blind
die Rüben	dee rewben	turnips
das Ruderboot	dass rooder-boat	rowing boat
rudern	roodern	to row
rund	roont	round
rutschen	rootshen	to slide
die Säcke	dee zeke(r)	sacks
die Säge	dee zehge(r)	saw
der Salat	derr zalaht	lettuce
die Sandburg	dee zant-boork	sand castle
der Satellit	derr zatelleet	satellite
die Schafe	dee shahfe(r)	sheep
der Schäfer	derr shayfer	shepherd
der Schäferhund	derr shayfer-hoont	sheepdog
die Schallplatten	dee shall-platten	records
der Schallplatten-spieler	der shall-platten-shpeeler	record player
die Schals	dee shahlz	scarves
schauen	showen	to look
schaukeln	showkeln	to swing
die Schere	dee shaire(r)	scissors
die Scheune	dee shoyne(r)	bcrn
die Schier	dee shee-er	skis
schießen	sheessen	to push, to shoot
das Schiff	dass shiff	ship
die Schiffskatze	dee shiffs-katse(r)	ship's cat
die Schiffs-schraube	dee shiffs-shrowbe(r)	propellor
die Schildkröte	dee shilt-kru(r)te(r)	tortoise
der Schinken	derr shinken	ham
die Schlafanzüge	dee shlahf-antsewge(r)	pyjamas
schlafen	shlahfen	to sleep
das Schlafzimmer	dass shlahf-tsimmer	bedroom
schlagen	shlahgen	to hit
die Schlangen	dee shlangen	snakes
der Schlepper	derr shlepper	tug boat
die Schleuse	dee shloyze(r)	lock
schließen	shleessen	to close
die Schlipse	dee shlipse(r)	ties
der Schlitten	derr shlitten	toboggan
Schlittschuh laufen	shlitt-shoolowfen	to skate
der Schlüssel	derr shlewssel	key
das Schlüsselloch	dass shlewssel-loch	keyhole
der Schmuck	derr shmook	jewellery
der Schmuggler	derr shmoogler	smuggler
der Schnee	derr shnay	snow
schneiden	shnyden	to cut
schnell	shnell	quickly
die Schnurrbärte	dee shnoor-bairte(r)	moustaches
die Schokolade	dee shokolahde(r)	chocolate
der Schornstein	derr shorn-shtyne	chimney, funnel
der Schrank	derr shrank	cupboard
der Schrauben-zieher	derr shrowben-tsee-er	screwdriver
schreiben	shryben	to write
die Schreib-maschine	dee shryp-masheene(r)	typewriter
der Schreibtisch	derr shryp-tish	desk
die Schublade	dee shoob-lahde(r)	drawer
die Schuhe	dee shoo-e(r)	shoes
die Schule	dee shoole(r)	school
der Schulhof	derr shool-hoaf	playground
der Schuppen	derr shoopen	shed
die Schürze	dee shewrtse(r)	apron
schwarz	shvarts	black
die Schweine	dee shvyne(r)	pigs
der Schweinestall	derr shvyne(r)-shtall	pigsty
das Schwert	dass shvairt	sword
schwimmen	shvimmen	to swim
der See	derr zay	lake
die Seehunde	dee zayhoonde(r)	seals
der Seetang	derr zaytank	sea weed
das Segelboot	dass zaygel-boat	sailing boat
sehen	zayen	to see
die Seife	dee zyfe(r)	soap
die Seilbahn	dee zyle-bahn	cable car
Seilchen springen	zyle-khen shpringen	to skip
die Sellerie	dee selleree	celery
der Sessel	derr zessel	arm chair
die Shorts	dee shorts	shorts
der Sicherheits-gurt	derr zikher-hyts-goort	safety belt
die Sicherheits-nadeln	dee zikher-hyts-nadeln	safety pins
sie	zee	her, she, them, they
der Silo	derr zeelo	silo
singen	zingen	to sing
der Sitz	derr zits	seat
sitzen	zitsen	to sit
die Socken	dee zoken	socks
die Sonne	dee zonne(r)	sun
die Sonnenbrillen	dee zonnen-brillen	sun glasses
der Sonnenschirm	derr zonnen-sheerm	beach umbrella, sunshade
der Spaten	derr shpahten	spade
der Spaziergang im All	derr shpatseer-gank im all	space walk
der Speck	derr shpek	bacon
der Speisesaal	derr shpyze(r)-zahl	dining room
der Spiegel	derr shpeegel	mirror
spitz	shpits	pointed
sprechen	shprekhen	to talk
springen	shpringen	to jump
der Spülstein	derr shpewl-shtyne	sink
das Stachel-schwein	dass shtachel-shvyne	porcupine
der Stall	derr shtall	stable
die Startbahn	dee shtart-bahn	runway
die Statue	dee shtahtoo-e(r)	statue
der Staubsauger	derr shtowp-zowger	vacuum cleaner
die Staumauer	dee shtow-mower	dam

German	Pronunciation	English
stehen	*shtayen*	to stand
steigen	*shtygen*	to climb
die Steine	*dee shtyne(r)*	stepping stones
die Sterne	*dee shtairne(r)*	stars
das Steuerruder	*dass shtoyer-rooder*	rudder
die Stewardess	*dee stewardess*	stewardess
die Stiefel	*dee shteefel*	boots
der Strand	*der shtrant*	beach
die Straße	*dee shtrahsse(r)*	road, street
die Strauße	*dee shtrowsse(r)*	ostriches
die Streichhölzer	*dee shtrykh-hu(r)ltser*	matches
stricken	*shtriken*	to knit
die Strickjacken	*dee shtrik-yaken*	cardigans
das Stroh	*dass shtroa*	straw
die Strumpf- hosen	*dee shtroompf-hoazen*	tights
der Stuhl	*derr shtool*	chair
das Stützgerüst	*dass shtewts-gerewst*	gantry
suchen	*zoochen*	to search
der Supermarkt	*derr zooper-markt*	supermarket
die Süßigkeiten	*dee zewssig-kyten*	sweets
das Tandem	*dass tandem*	tandem
der Tanker	*derr tanker*	tanker
der Tankwagen	*derr tank-vahgen*	fuel tanker
tanzen	*tantsen*	to dance
die Taschen	*dee tashen*	pockets
die Taschenlampe	*dee tashenlampe(r)*	torch
das Taschen- messer	*dass tashenmesser*	penknife
der Taschen- rechner	*derr tashen-rekhner*	calculator
die Taschentücher	*dee tashen-tewkher*	hand- kerchiefs
die Tassen	*dee tassen*	cups
das Taxi	*dass taxi*	taxi
der Teich	*derr tykh*	pond
das Telefon	*dass telefoan*	telephone
das Teleskop	*dass teleskoap*	telescope
die Teller	*dee teller*	plates
der Teppich	*derr teppikh*	carpet
der Tiger	*derr teeger*	tiger
der Tisch	*derr tish*	table
die Toilette	*dee toilette(r)*	toilet
die Tomate	*dee tomate(r)*	tomato
das Tonbandgerät	*dass toanbant-gerayt*	tape recorder
die Töpfe	*dee tu(r)pfe(r)*	saucepans
die Topfpflänzen	*dee topf-pflentsen*	plants
das Tor	*dass tor*	gate
tragen	*trahgen*	to carry
die Tragfläche	*dee trahk-flekhe(r)*	wing
das Tragflächen- boot	*dass trahk-flekhen-boat*	hydrofoil
der Traktor	*derr traktor*	tractor
die Trauben	*dee trowben*	grapes
traurig	*trowrik*	sadly
die Treppe	*dee treppe(r)*	stairs
der Treppenabsatz	*derr treppen-apzats*	landing
das Treppenhaus	*dass treppen-howss*	stairwell
treten	*trayten*	to kick
trinken	*trinken*	to drink
die T-shirts	*dee tee-shirts*	tee-shirts
der Tukan	*derr tookahn*	toucan
der Tunnel	*derr toonel*	tunnel
der Türknopf	*derr tewrn-knopf*	door handle

German	Pronunciation	English
über	*ewber*	over
das U-Boot	*dass oo-boat*	submarine
die Uhr	*dee oor*	clock
die Umhänge	*dee oom-henge(r)*	cloaks
die Uniformen	*dee ooniformen*	uniforms
unter	*oonter*	under
die Untertassen	*dee oontertassen*	saucers
die Verbände	*dee ferbende(r)*	bandages
der Verbands- kasten	*derr ferbants-kasten*	first-aid kit
verfolgen	*ferfolgen*	to chase
sich verstecken	*zikh fershteken*	to hide
die Vogelscheuche	*dee foagel-shoykhe(r)*	scarecrow
vor	*for*	in front of
die Vorhänge	*dee for-henge(r)*	curtains
der Vorratsraum	*derr for-rahts-rowm*	store room
der Wald	*derr valt*	forest
die Walze	*dee valtse(r)*	roller
warten	*varten*	to wait
der Wärter	*derr vehrter*	keeper
waschen	*vashen*	to wash
die Wasch- maschine	*dee vash-masheene(r)*	washing machine
ins Wasser springen	*inss vasser shpringen*	to dive
der Wasserfall	*derr vasser-fall*	waterfall
die Wasserkresse	*dee vasser-kresse(r)*	watercress
der Wasserski- läufer	*derr vasser-shee-loyfer*	water skier
der Wassertrog	*derr vasser-troak*	water trough
der Wecker	*derr veker*	alarm clock
der Wegweiser	*derr vayg-vyzer*	sign post
der Wein	*derr vyne*	wine
weiß	*vyss*	white
der Weltraum	*derr velt-rowm*	space
werfen	*vairfen*	to throw
um die Wette laufen	*oom dee vette(r) lowfen*	to race
wild	*vilt*	fiercely
die Winde	*dee vinde(r)*	winch
die Windmühle	*dee vint-mewle(r)*	windmill
wir	*veer*	we
der Wissen- schaftler	*derr vissen-shaftler*	scientist
der Wohnwagen	*derr voan-vahgen*	caravan
der Wolf	*derr volf*	wolf
das Wrack	*dass vrak*	wreck
die Würstchen	*dee vewrst-khen*	sausages
wütend	*vewtent*	angrily
der Zaun	*derr tsown*	fence
das Zebra	*dass tsaybra*	zebra
die Zelte	*dee tselte(r)*	tents
die Ziege	*dee tseege(r)*	goat
die Ziegelsteine	*dee tseegel-shtyne(r)*	bricks
ziehen	*tsee-en*	to pull
die Zitronen	*dee tsitroanen*	lemons
der Zoll	*derr tsoll*	customs
der Zucker	*derr tsooker*	sugar
der Zug	*derr tsook*	train
die Zwiebeln	*dee tsvee-beln*	onions
zwischen	*tsvishen*	between

Pronunciation Guide

On these pages is the guide on how to say all the sentences in German in this book, using the same rules as on page 40.

Page 4 and 5 Inspektor Nomen und die geheimnisvollen Vorgänge auf dem Markt.
inspektor nomen oont dee gehymniss-follen forgenge(r) owf daym markt.
nomen gayt owf dayn markt, oom eynen deep tsoo finden.
err denkt: "vair ist dee keershen oont dee aird-bairen oont dee himbairen?"
err zeet zikh eyne(r) ananas an, lest eyne(r) meloane(r) fallen oont ist eynen apfel.
err gayt an dayn oronjen, dayn tsitroanen oont dayn aprikoazen forbye.
err showt dee beernen, dee trowben oont dee bananen an.
err blypt shtayen, oom owf eynen pfeerzikh tsoo drewken oont oom eyn pampelmōōze(r) oont eyne pahr pflowmen tsoo kowfen.
"vair hat dee airpsen oont dee boanen oont dayn zalaht gegessen?"
nomen oonterzōōcht dee kartoffeln oont dee muren oont dee koalku(r)pfe(r).
err tritt owf eyne(r) tomate(r), shtu(r)st eyne ku(r)p-khen foller piltse(r) oont eynen eymer mit vasserkresse(r) oom.
err showt hinter dayn rōōben oont daym roasenkoal hairfor oont kreekht an derr roaten bayte(r) forbye
err gayt an derr selleree forbye, oont zeet zikh dee radeez-khen oont dee tsveebeln an.
err rootsht owf eyner shtange(r) porray owss, shtolpert ewber eynen blōōmen-koal oont findet dee deebe(r).

Page 6 and 7 Inspektor Nomen und die geshtoalenen Diamanten
inspektor nomen oont dee geshtoalenen dee-amanten
inspektor nomen fehrt tsoo daym shiff. err gayt dass fallreep hinowf oont shpricht mit daym kapitayn.
derr kapitayn ertsaylt eem, dass eynige(r) dee-amanten fon eynem deep geshtoalen vorden zint. ahber eyne(r) frow hat een gezayen.
nomen shlykht ewber dass deck oont fenkt dayn mann. ahber syne(r) tashen zint lehr.
derr deep hat dee dee-amanten owf daym shiff fershtekt. kannst doo zee finden?

Page 8 and 9 Wachtmeister Verb hat einen schweren Tag
vacht-myster fairp hat eynen shvairen tahk
fairp leekt im bett oont shlayft. err vacht owf oont shtykt owss daym bett.
err drayt dee vasser-krehne(r) owf, vesht zikh dee hende(r) oont rypt zyne gezikht troken.
err pootst zikh dee tsayne(r), tseet zynen shlahf-antsook owss, tseet zyne(r) klydoonk an oont bewrstet zikh dass hahr
fairp rootsht dass gelender hinoonter oont ist dann zyne frew-stewk.
err trinkt zynen kafay, leest dee tsytoonk oont lest eynen teller fallen.
err fewtert dayn kanahr-ee-en foagel, shleest dass fenster oont u(r)fnet dee tewr.
err fehrt mit zynem vahgen, gayt inss bewro oont shrypt eynen breef.
err shpricht am telefoan, err-tsaylt nomen fon eynen rowp-ewberfall oont loyft hinowss tsoo zynem vahgen.
err showt zikh eyn fenster an, zeet eynen fōōss-shtapfen oont zōōcht dayn eyne-brekher.
fairp verfolkt dayn eyne-brekher, fenkt een oont zee gerahten in eyne hant-gemenge(r).
derr eyne-brekher tritt fairp, fairp shlaykt dayn eyne-brekher, oont err fellt oom.
fairp haypt een owf, nimmt een tsoor politsye-vache(r) oont shpairt een eyne.

Page 10 Inspektor Nomen und der priesgekrönte Bulle
inspektor nomen oond derr pryz-gekru(r)nte(r) boole(r)
drye doome(r) deebe(r) ferzōōchen, eynen pryz-gekru(r)nten boolen tsoo shtaylen. doorch velkhe(r) tore(r) gayt inspektor nomen, oom zee tsoo ertappen?

Page 12 und 13 Inspektor Nomen und die Fabrikspione
inspektor nomen oont dee fabreek-shpee-oane(r)
nomen shtayt drowssen for eyner fabreek vacher. err zeeht, vee tsvye spee-oane(r) herowss-lowfen.
err folkt eenen dee shtrahsse(r) hinoonter, doorch dass tor hindoorch oont in dayn park hineyne.

err loyft an daym zay, an dayn showkeln oont an derr marsh-kappele(r) forb; dee shpee-oane(r) zint bye eyne(r) shōōle(r).
nomen blickt doorch dass gitter oont zeet zee owf daym shōōl-hoaf.
err ferfolkt zee an derr keerkhe(r) forbye, oom dass keeno heroom oont in dass hoatel hineyne.
err findet dee shpee-oane(r) in eynem kafay. dann gayen zee tsoo derr amper oont ewber-kvairen dee shtrahsee(r) an daym fōōssgenger-ewbergank.
zee varten an eyner booss-halte-shtelle(r). nomen loyft hinter eynen latairnen-pfahl oont fershtekt zikh hinter eyner shtahtoo-e(r).
dee shpee-oane(r) ferpassen dayn booss oont gayen tsoo fōōss vyter an daym kranken-howss oont an eynem loch in derr shtrahsse(r) forbye.
zee zayen daym mann mit eynem press-looft-hammer tsoo, vairfen eynen blik owf eynen bagger oont eynen valtse(r).
zee shpringen ewber eynige(r) roaren oont tseegelshtyne(r). dah zayen zee nomen mit eynem politsisten.
zee rennen in eyn bewro, dass treppen-howss hinowf oont owf dee foyer-lyte nomen ferfolkt zee bis owf dass dach, oom eynen fahnenmast heroom oont ervisht zee shleesslikh bye eynem shorn-shtyne.

Page 14 and 15 Inspektor Nomen fliegt mit eine Düsenmaschine
inspektor nomen fleekt mit eyner dewzen-masheene(r)
inspektor nomen fehrt tsoom flōōk-hahfen. err ist owf derr zōōche(r) nach eynem shmoogler.
err tsykt syne(r) flōōk-karte(r) for. err gayt doorch dayn tsoll oont lest synen pass ap-shtempeln.
err vartet in derr ap-flōōk halle(r), err bekommt zyne(r) board-karte(r). err zeet zikh dee anderen passajeerer an.
inspektor nomen gayt tsoor dewzen-masheene(r) hinowss. err gayt doorch dass flōōk-tsoyk bis tsoo eynem zits. err befestikt zynen zikher-hyts-gōōrt.
dee dewsen-masheene(r) rollt ewber dee shtart-bahn oont errhaypt zikh in dee looft.
err shpricht mit daym peeloaten, veerft eynen blik owf dass instroomenten-brett oont gayt veeder tsoo-rewk dayn gank entlank.
err zeet dee golt-barren, darowfhin flewstert err derr stewardess etvas inss oar oont ferhaftet dayn shmoogler.

Page 16 Inspektor Nomen und der Kostümverleih
inspektor nomen oont derr kostewm-ferlye
nomen oont syne assistent gay-en tsoo eynem kostewm-ferlye. vee-feele(r) kostewme(r) probeeren zee an?

Page 18 and 19: Nomen und die Supermarktbande
nomen oont dee supermarktbande(r)
nomen gayt tsoom supermarkt. err ist owf derr zōōche(r) nach laybens-mittel-deeben.
err gayt am broat oont an derr booter forbye oont zeet zikh dayn kayze(r) an.
err gayt an derr milkh oont am yogōōrt forbye oont lest eynige(r) eyer fallen.
err zeet dayn shinken oont dayn shpek an oont kreekht am fish forbye.
err blikt hinter dass mehl oont dayn tsooker oont dee shokolade(r).
err shtayt byme hoanik, showt zikh dee marmelade(r) an oont zōōcht zikh eyne pahr zewssig-kyten owss.
err loyft an dayn kōōchen oont plets-khen forbye oont macht eynen groassen shritt ewber dee bru(r)-khen.
err shtu(r)st doazen oont flashen oont glayser oom. err rōōt zikh bye derr gefreertrōō-e(r) owss, tritt mit daym fōōss gaygen eynem korp oond eynige(r) kartoanz.
nomen findet etvas flysh, eyne hewn-khen oont mairere(r) vewrst-khen.
err loyft an dayn kassen forbye, shprinkt ewber eyne pahr eyne-kowfs-tashen oont ewber eynige(r) zecke(r).
dann ervisht err dee deebe(r) err layt zee in eynen eyne-kowfs-vahgen oont brinkt zee inss hoonde(r)-gefengnis.

Page 20 Detektiv Präposition und das Gespensterschloß
daytekteef prepozit-see-oan oont dass geshpenster-shloss
daytekteef prepozit-see-oan gayt tsoo daym shloss. dort hahben gowner eynen shats fershtekt.
err kommt am vasser-grahben an, gayt ewber dee tsōōk-brewke(r) oont oonter daym tor-boagen hindoorch.
err showt oonter eynen shtyne, zōōcht mit syner tashenlampe(r) nach daym shats oont loykhtet tsvishen tsvye kanoanen.
alss err bye eyner zoyle(r) shtayen blypt, hurt err shritte(r) inn derr naye(r) oont showt in eynem rowm.
eyne geshpenst errshynt hinter eem, oont dann shtayt es for eem. err loyft owf dee treppe(r) tsoo.
err shprinkt shnell hinoonter, fellt doorch dayn fōōss-boaden, landet yedoch owf synen fewssen.

Page 21 Pronomen kommt zur Hilfe
pronomen kommt tsoor hilfe(r)

lss prepozit-see-oon nikht tsoo-rewk-kommt, fairt daytekteef pronomen
soo daym geshpenster-shloss.
zee gayt doorch dass tor, rooft: "vo bist doo?" oont zoocht een.
dann zeet zee, dass err in dass ferleess gefallen ist.
hilf meer, bitte(r)" zahkt err. "ikh tsee dikh herowss," zahkt zee.
'shnell, veer mewssen oonss fershteken. zee kommen heer heroonter oont
vairden oonss zayen.
veer hahben een geefoonden," zahgen dee gowner. plu(r)ts-likh zayen dee
owner zee, ahber pronomen ferhalftet zee.

Page 22 Inspektor Nomen und die Entführer
inspektor nomen oont dee entfewrer
eynes nachts shlikhen tsayn shpee-oune(r) in eyne hotel, oom eynen
berewmten vissen-shaftler tsoo entfewren.
alls zee inspektor nomen kommen hu(r)ten, fershtekten zee zikh. kannst doo
zee alle(r) finden?

Page 24 and 25 Inspektor Nomen verfolgt die Gauner
inspektor nomen ferfolkt dee gowner
tsvye gowner entkommen owss daym gefengnis. nomen loyft hinter eenen
hair.
zee fahren owf eynem tandem dafon. nomen ferfolkt zee owf eynem fahr-
raht.
zee shpringen owf eynen roller. nomen folkt eenen owf roll-shoo-en
dee gowner shtaylen eyne owto. nomen helt eyne taxi an.
zee entkommen in eynem last-vahgen. nomen fehrt mit eynem leefer-vahgen
hinter eenen hair.
dee gowner hayben in einem flook-tsoyg ap. nomen ferfolkt zee in eynem
hoop-shrowber.
zee shvayben an eynem fallsheerm herap. nomen landet in eynem balloan.
zee shtygen in eynen tsook. nomen yahkt zee in eynem renn-vahgen.
zee shtaylen eyne motoar-boat. nomen folkt eenen in eynem zaygel-boat.
zee shpringen in eyne rooder-boat. nomen paddelt in eynem kanoo hinter
eenen hair.
zee shtaylen eynen pfairde(r)-transporter. nomen veerd fon eyner foyer-vair
mitgenommen.
zee hahben eynen oonfall owf eynem motoar-raht. nomen fenkt zee oont
transporteert zee in eynem kranken-vahgen ap.

Page 26 Die Schule für Verbdetektive
dee shoole(r) fewr fairp-daytekteefe(r)
heer zayen veer feele(r) fairben in eyner shoole(r) fewr daytekteefe(r).
kannst doo dee zechs gowner ent-deken, dee zee be-obachten?

Page 28 Detektiv Adverb und der Fleischdeib
daytekteef adfairp oont derr flysh-deep
eyness ahbents beobachtete(r) daytekteef adfairp, vee eyne mann flysh
shtahl. err zah folgendess:
eyne hoont leef langsam dahair oont shnewfelte(r) lowt nach essen. dann
zetste(r) err zikh trowrik hin.
plu(r)tslikh shtahl eyne mann etvas flysh, oont derr hoont hatte(r) es balt
owfgefressen. err vackelte(r) glewklikh mit daym shvants.
derr mann shtrykhelte(r) dayn hoont leebefoll. derr metsger shimpfte(r)
vewtent, oont derr mann leef shnell davon.
derr hoont bellte(r) vee vilt. der metsger ervishte(r) een fast ahber err leef
ayben-fallss davon.

Page 29 Detektiv Adjektivs Bericht
daytekteef adyekteefs berikht
daytekteef adyekteef zah dayn hoont oont dayn mann. zee be-shrypt zee
folgender-mahssen.
derr hoont hatte(r) eynen dewnen kopf, shpitse(r) oaren oont browne(r)
owgen.
err hatte(r) eyne shvartsess fell, eynen langen shvants oont eyne roatess
halssbant.
derr mann hatte(r) eyne roondess gesikht, lokige(r) hahre(r) oont eyne
growen bart.
err trook eynen grewnen hoot, eynen alten mantel oont eyne vyssess hemt.
err trook eyne(r) blowe(r) hoaze(r), gelbe(r) zoken oont groasse(r) shteefel.

Page 30 and 31 Inspektor Nomen und die Schmuggler
inspektor nomen oont dee shmoogler
inspektor nomen lowert shmooglern owf. err vill herowssfinden vo eer
fershtek ist.
err zeet eyne motoar-boat oont beobachtet dee shmoogler. err folkt eenen
dayn shtrant entlank.
zee gayen an ayner zant-boork forbye, trayten gaygen eynen eymer oont
shtoassen eynen zonnen-sheerm oom.
eyner tritt owf eynen shpahten, eyne anderer gaygen eynen ball. dee

shmoogler laygen eyne(r) pikniks-powze(r) eyne.
nomen zitst owf dayn keezel-shtynen err haypt eynen kreps owf oont zetst
een in eynen felzen-tewmpel.
err folkt dayn mennern bis tsoo dayn felzen, rootsht owf etvas zay-tank owss
oont errykht dayn loykht-toorm.
err klettert owf dee klippe(r), kreekht in eynen toonel oont findet dass
fershterk derr shmoogler in eyner hu(r)le(r).

Page 32 and 33 Inspektor Nomen in Gefahr
inspektor nomen in gefahr
nomen findet dee shmoogler in eerer hu(r)le(r). ahber zee bemerken, dass
err allyne ist oont machen zikh daran, een tsoo ferfolgen.
err rennt vayg eyne(r) shtrahsse(r) hinoonter, ewber-kvairt eyne(r)
brewkve(r) oont errykht eine(e) kroytsoonk.
nomen blypt shtayen, oom eynen vayg-vyzer tsoo layzen, loyft vyter eynen
pfaht hinap oont kreekht doorch eyne(r) hecke(r).
err loyft owf eyne pahr boyme(r) tsoo. dann kommt err an eynen flooss oont
paddelt owf eynem floass tsoom anderen oofer.
mit mewe(r) rettet err zikh for eynem vasserfall, eylt eynen hewgel hinowf
oont shprinkt ewber eynen tsown.
nomen blypt an eynem kanahl shtayen, shprinkt owf eynen kahn oont
shtykt an eyner shloyze(r) veeder ap.
nomen klettert ewber eyne tor, rennt an eyne pahr tselten forbye oont
shtolpert ewber eyne(r) lyne(r).
err rennt vyter an eynem voan-vahgen forbye, errykht eynen bach oont
balanseert ewber dee shtyne(r) anss andere(r) oofer.
err eylt ewber eyne(r) shtow-mower, an eyner vint-mewle(r) forbye oont in
eynen valt hineyne.
err klettert owf eynen berk, fehrt mit eyner zyle-bahn oont tritt hinowss in
dayn shnay.
err probeert eyne pahr shee-er an, rodelt owf eynem shlitten dayn hank
hinoonter oont klettert ewber eyne(r) mower.
err loyft in eynen doonklen rowm oont knipst dass likht an. dee shmoogler
zint eem owf einer politsye-vache in dee falle(r) gegangen.

Page 34 and 35 Inspektor Nomen im Zoo
inspektor nomen im tsoa
im tsoa ist derr li(r)ve(r) owss zynem kayfik owss-gebrochen. velkhem pfat
folkt nomen, oom een tsoo finden?

Page 36 and 37 Inspektor Nomen sucht nach Anhaltspunkten
inspektor nomen zoocht nach anhalts-poonkten
nomen u(r)fnet dee tewr tsoo zynem bewro. "heer vahr yaymant," denkt
err oont macht zikh owf dee zooche nach anhalts-poonkten.
err betrachtet dayn fooss-boaden, entdekt eyne(r) offene(r) shoop-lahde(r)
oont haypt eyne(r) arm-bant-oor owf.
err findet eynen shloossel oont eyne tashen-tooch oont eyne(r) tashen-
lampe(r).
eergent-yaymant hat synen fewl-fayder-halter benootst, eyne(r)
breef-marke(r) geshtoalen oont eynen breef-oom-shlank ge-u(r)fnet.
yaymant hat zyne notits-booch gelayzen, mit zynem komputer geshpeelt
oont zynen tashen-rechner fallen lassen.
yaymant hat zynen blyshtift doorch-gebrochen, zyne getrenk owss-
getroonken oont in zyne booter-broat gebissen.
dann zeet err in zynen shrank oont findet dayn eyne-brekher.

Page 38 and 39 Inspektor Nomen fängt einen Weltraumspion
inspektor nomen fenkt eynen velt-rowm-shpee-oan
nomen kommt gerahde(r) in daym moment am rowmfahrt-tsentroom an,
alss eyne(r) rakayte(r) apgeshossen veerd. err vyss, dass eyne shpee-oan an
boart ist.
err tseet eynen rowm-antsook an oont trifft tsvye astro-nowten dee een
tsoor apshoos-rampe(r) bringen.
err shtykt in dass rowmshiff, laykt zikh owf eyne(r) leege(r), oont dee
rakayte(r) haypt ap.
err zeet dee airde(r) oonter zikh oont blikt owf dee zonne(r) oont dee
stairne(r).
err sheest an eyner rowm-faire(r), eynem zatelleeten oont eyner rowm-
shtatsee-oan forbye.
nomen landet owf dayn moant. dee andere(r) rakayte(r) ist shoan dah.
err fairt mit eynem moant-fahr-tsoyk, bemairkt fooss-shtapfen im moant-
shtowp oont fenkt dayn shpee-oan hinter eynem broken moant-geshtyne.
err fleekt tsoo-rewk in dayn velt-rowm. eyne may-tee-oar trifft dee rowm-
kapsel. nomen macht eyne shpatseer-gank im all.
err repareert dee antenne(r). dee rowm-kapsel kairt in dee airt-oomlowf-
bahn tsoo-rewk oont landet im mair.
zee klettern owss derr eyne-shteeks-looke(r). froshmenner shtayen beryt.
oom eenen tsoo helfen. dee miss-ee-oan ist tsoo eynem zikheren ende(r)
gekommen.